The 20 Types
Of

Bitches
In The World

By Tonya Love

I0415578

Table of Contents

Chapter 1

It doesn't matter where you live, your level of education, your race or nationality, you can rest assured that there is either one specific type of bitch, or a combination of these types, living among you. Some people may see the word "bitch" as some sort of derogatory term and immediately disregard anyone or anything associated with the word. However, as a woman, I know about the different types of bitches that exist in the world because most of them have crossed my path at one time or another. Bitches are everywhere. You may try to escape or avoid them, but it's almost impossible because they're like roaches: they will survive and they will not die! Although it is true that bitches come in all species, there are 20 main types that every man, woman, and child should be able to identity whenever possible.

The Rich Bitch

What constitutes "rich" is as much a state of mind as it is economics. Although being "rich" is relative, a rich bitch usually tends to be a woman who has assets, or she has access, to millions of dollars. Her wealth contributes to and exemplifies her behavior. Whatever she wants, this bitch finds a way to get it. She has money dripping out of her lip gloss and, in most cases, only needs a man to supply her sexual needs. Vanity is of upmost importance to her. Everything she wears has to be of designer quality and reflect her status. From her Prada eyewear to her Valentino pumps, this chick has to have them.

If she finds too many other females in her echelon rocking the same wears, she will shift brands in a heartbeat to remain as "exclusive" as possible. She dines at "reservation only" restaurants; she only flies first class, or even better, in a private jet and she will not settle for lesser accommodations.   Depending upon whether her wealth is inherited or if she earns her money will sometimes affects her spending practices. For instance, if she didn't have to lift a finger for a penny of her wealth, she tends to act more like a rich bitch on steroids. Impulsive Mercedes Benz purchases are her modus operandi. If she has to work for her "benjamins", she will tend to use a little more discretion with how she spends her money.

Trust fund bitches tend to be a bit lazier than working rich bitches. Her trust fund allows her the means to not have to lift a finger in life unless she desires to. A rich bitch's age has an effect on her behavior. Young rich bitches love Starbucks and Abercrombie. They are in the mall at 9:59 am on Saturday morning with their mothers' or they are with groups of their snobby teen friends. Their money spending is focused on clothes, shoes, makeup, handbags, and electronics. A teen rich bitch carries little cash and she uses her parents' credit cards to make her purchases. She'll spend the whole day swiping her father's American Express card, then turn around and complain to her other rich friends about how she doesn't have anything to wear to the game on Friday night.

The middle aged rich bitch has broader ways to spend her cash. She is buying mansions and luxury cars. Her education and life experiences allow her to make costlier acquisitions. She begins to take notice of the finer things in life, like expensive art and classical music. Now, instead of using her parents' credit card, that American Express is in her name. She may even participate in expensive hobbies and sports (golf, lacrosse, horseback riding, etc.)

Lastly, there is the old rich bitch. If living an extravagant life hasn't gotten the best of this bitch, she tends to be the epitome of refinement and culture. She loves her Grey Poupon and all 6 of her dogs. Oftentimes she's married, but if she isn't, that does not stop her from buying her man. If she is buying him, you can bet he's at least 20 years her junior, is fit, and barely speaks any English. Her main activities revolve around traveling to exotic parts of the world and spending her money indulging in anything that makes her feel comfortable. Instead of buying homes, the old rich bitch spends her money being philanthropic, donating to charities, and on any activities that involve exposing her socialite status.

The Broke Bitch

This is probably the worst kind of bitch. She's the worse because not only is she broke, she's also likely to be angry, and her anger fuels her behavior. She is always robbing Peter to pay Paul.   Most broke bitches have either low paying jobs or no job at all. She spends her time trying to survive on very little money and with the help of government assistance.

Utility bills are disconnected from time to time, and she uses her children's Social Security numbers to get them turned on. Her cable is turning off for months at least twice a year, and she sometimes has difficulty keeping her cell phone in service. She doesn't have a checking account or credit cards, everything is paid using a pre-paid debit card. Home ownership is not an option because of her bad credit, so she remains a lifelong renter. Despite her financial situation, there are many broke bitches that love and will find a way to look good. Many broke bitches love to shop. She'll search the mall looking for that kiosk that specializes in selling the really good knockoff designer handbags. She might even spend a lot of money on a pair of shoes or an authentic designer bag, but rest assured, her outfit costs more than what is available on her debit card. Broke bitches tend to be overweight or in overall bad health. Sitting at home all day, eating cheap food, and watching Judge Mathis, Judge Judy, The Jerry Springer and Maury Povich shows on television, creates a perfect storm for being big and broke.

When she gets to the point to where her weight affects her ability to breathe and realizes she can't even afford a gym membership, she'll fall into a deeper depression and eat even more.

Broke bitches have a bad habit of attracting broke men. He is sure to be just as uneducated and as unmotivated as she. A faithful man is hard to find, but a man that is faithful to a broke bitch just does not exist. He is always on the lookout to upgrade his lifestyle and he is a master at keeping his options open.

Oftentimes, the broke bitch will settle for men who are prone to engage in criminal activities. She will spend her last dime bailing her man out of jail or putting money on his commissary tab. Most of her time is spent figuring out ways to survive on very little financial support from the man in her life. If she has children, she is lazy about pursuing her child's father for child support because she believes that the $13 a month check is not worth the hassle of taking him to court.

Being a broke bitch is also generational. Women will pattern themselves to all the other women around them. In as much as being "rich" is a state of mind, so is being "broke". The mind of a broke bitch functions within a lower realm of energy and material. She tends to not expect much out of life and, in turn, she receives very little from it. In order to avoid living this lifestyle, broke young bitches have to start making wiser decisions. Spending less time chasing boys and popularity, and spending more time getting an education to acquire a self-sustaining career are key ways to turning their lives around. The good news for broke bitches is that, with a little effort, they do not have to necessarily stay that way.

The Crazy Bitch

This type of bitch is the one that most people like to stay far away from and avoid like the plague. She acts deranged, is mentally unstable, and probably should be on some form of psychotropic medication. These types always are in some form of conflict and everything is an emergency. She requires a lot of attention and energy. A man, or her friends, definitely want to eat a steady diet of Wheaties and spinach messing around with this chick.

Her craziness is almost always an overreaction to the smallest problems or situations. If she's in public with her man and they encounter a co-worker of his, the crazy bitch will have an unprovoked hissy fit and accuse him of sleeping with the co-worker. She doesn't base her beliefs on clear proof because everything is based off of her "feelings". All he has to do is say, "Hi!!" and all hell will break loose. If the co-worker is even slightly attractive, a crazy bitch will spend the next week trying to access as much information as she can on the co-worker, hoping she can find enough evidence to prove that they are messing around!

She is relentless and stubborn; once she gets an idea in her head, there is no changing it. Her man is always on pins and needles around her because he doesn't want her to even have the idea that he is possibly cheating on her with another woman. For peace's sake, he hates to even make eye contact with other females for fear of having to argue about a secret lover that just doesn't exist. The crazy bitch is usually extremely violent. She cannot keep her hands to herself and will find a reason to smack her man in the face on any given day. She gets a kick out of cutting up his furniture, keying his car, and bleaching his favorite jeans. When she's angry, she'll do anything she can do to hurt him and she will spend a ton of time conjuring up ways to make his life miserable.

The interesting thing about a crazy bitch is when she's not angry, her behavior is the extreme opposite. It is amazing to see how incredibly loving a crazy bitch is when she is not experiencing one of her episodes. One minute she's fixing her man breakfast in bed; the next minute, she's throwing the breakfast dishes at him because he got called in to work early. She is a true and living example of a Dr. Jekyll and Mr. Hyde. In psychiatric terms, she could be diagnosed with suffering from a bipolar or manic depressive disorder. If she's not taking medications to help level her mood swings, she probably should be.

In truth, most women like this find it hard to maintain steady relationships with men or anybody else for that matter. She may have a gorgeous face and a killer body, but once her man is exposed to her fits of emotional instability, he tends to make a swift exit out of the relationship. There are so many drop dead "dimes" in the world who are single and lonely.

These are probably some of the craziest acting lunatics walking the planet and the sad part is, most of them don't even realize that they're nuts. Ask any crazy bitch if SHE believes she's a crazy bitch, her answer will likely be an emphatic, "No!" She believes she is perfectly sane and that the person accusing her of insanity is the one that needs to have their head examined. Surprisingly, not all crazy bitches are lonely though. There are a segment of population of men who love dealing with this type of woman, partly because they enjoy the emotional gymnastics these women expose them to. Every day is a new adventure and he enjoys the excitement that her mood swings brings to their relationship. In many ways, the men that love crazy bitches are, no doubt, crazy themselves.

Chapter 2

The Real Bitch

The real bitch is the one who freely acknowledges her condition in life and is swift in letting those around her know what is on her mind. She speaks the truth, no matter who likes it or who doesn't like it. There is no respect given to taking a person's feelings into consideration when dealing with this type of bitch. She takes pride in expressing her views on any given subject, everybody will know where she stands, and how she feels. I had the pleasure of having had a real bitch as my college roommate. She was direct, clear, and one of the most honest people I've ever had the opportunity to know. I believe that one of the main factors that allows a real bitch to be so brazen is that she tends to be confident and secure in herself and her ideas. Whether she is spot on correct or dead wrong, she has confidence in how she maneuvers through life. If she only can afford to drive a Ford, then that's probably the type of car you'll see a real bitch driving. If she can only afford to shop at Marshalls' for shoes, then Marshalls' shoes are the only shoes you'll see a real bitch rocking. With her, it's less about brand names and more about quality products.

Dealing with a real bitch is easy because her realness also exudes trustworthiness. She is a great friend and will have come to the aid, or defense, of anyone she considers to be a friend. She is the ear that will listen to her man (and her friends) and never share a word of their conversations with anyone else. It's pretty easy to win an argument with a real bitch. She will admit when she's wrong and she may even apologize for her actions because it's no skin off her back in doing so.

On the flipside of her loyalty, the real bitch will implode on anybody who betrays her or anyone that she loves. She will not bite her tongue or show any mercy to anyone that she identifies as a traitor. Telling it like it is has a whole new meaning when communicated through the mouth of the real bitch. What makes her so confident is the fact that she is also a strong and courageous individual. She can hold her own weight both physically and mentally. She is not afraid to beat anybody's ass and she may even be willing to take an ass whooping if she's fighting for what she believes in. If she's involved with a man that cheats on her, her unwillingness to live in denial of her situation will cause her to make whatever changes necessary to retain happiness in her life. If that means being without a man until the right one comes along, then that's what she is willing to do.

A real bitch deals with life's challenges head on and she is deliberate. Nothing is left to chance and she is careful not to repeat past mistakes. This is why a real bitch tends to have successful and lasting relationships. Being real is synonymous with being true. True friends will last forever, true love will last forever, true intentions are pure, and the list goes on and on. Let's not assume that all real bitches are faithful, some do cheat on their men. The cheating real bitch will admit her wrongs when she is caught and suffer whatever consequences of her cheating. The overlapping theme still remains true. Even though she cheats, her man may be inclined to stay with her because the one thing he can count on is her "realness". He can count on the fact that, despite her flaws, she is not an arch deceiver and out to destroy him. A real bitch supplies a certain amount of security to a man and this security is a primary reason why men love this type of bitch.

The Fake Bitch

A fake bitch is the opposite of a real bitch in almost every way imaginable. Everything, from her appearance to her personality, is misleading and flat out false. It's easy to spot a fake bitch from a mile away. She is consumed by her looks which always must be in line with a standard that she deems is acceptable. For instance, a fake bitch usually has to have something fake about her body. In many cases, everything about her is fake. She has fake hair, fake nails, fake eyelashes, even her jewelry is fake. She feels uncomfortable living in her own skin. If she has some discretionary cash, she will invest her money on plastic surgery getting fake teeth, a fake nose, fake breasts, and even a fake ass. Many fake bitches look plastic and unnatural, yet they desire real men!

Aside from having sexual relations, real men have a hard time finding anything in common with fake bitches. Men will call them up at 2 a.m. for a booty call, but as soon as the sun rises, these same men don't want to be seen in public with a fake looking bitch. Not all fake bitches are unattractive though. Some do work that fake magic quite beautifully. A good weave goes a long way in making a fake bitch look real and natural looking additions can accent her looks quite beautifully. But for the majority of fakes, she tends to look like a hot mess. If she does have a man or is married, fake bitches are extremely expensive mates. Her man has to spend and make sure she has the money for all the hair, nails, and pedicure appointment needs.

Her fake persona is not just limited to the physical. It also manifests itself through her personality. Truthfulness and trustworthiness are not the normal character traits of fake bitches. She lives in her own dream world and has to lie to herself, and other people, in order to feel secure in her world. She creates a façade to live out a fantasy of her life that just does not exist. Fake bitches will lie about having a degree, where they work, how much money they make, and even lie about having a man.

Her life is a true mystery, filled with exaggerations and half-truths. A fake bitch's own family members have a hard time interacting with her on a daily basis. They see what she pretends to be to people on the outside, all the while knowing what the truth is underneath the lies. There are some instances where fake bitches are such skilled liars that they have everybody in their sphere completely fooled. Over time, they become masterful at the craft of creating the illusion of themselves. This

Illusion becomes their reality and becomes more and more believable over time.

This is why old fake bitches are more believable than the young ones. Overall, the best way for a woman to avoid being fake and phony is for her to just simply be her authentic self. For some, this is a difficult thing to be because everything on television or in music rebukes originality. The constant battle between being someone else or accepting self is a battle the fake bitch loses every time.

The Hoe Bitch

What are some of the main attributes of a hoe bitch? A hoe bitch is a woman who has little to no regard for the man (or woman) she opens her legs up to. She just likes to have sex. Any and all kinds of sexual activities is what she focuses on throughout her day. She does not discriminate and is not particular or picky about her partners. As long as he has a shlong and he's willing to use it, she is game for anything. Hoes are not always easily identifiable. Sometimes, it's hard to judge whether or not a woman is a hoe by just merely looking at her. Some women are overt hoes while some are undercover hoes. The overt hoes are the ones that let you know within 3 minutes of conversation with her that she's happily willing to bang. No flirtation is needed, no subtle talk, and no beating around the bush. This woman's sexual appetite is salacious and hard to quench.

The undercover hoe is not as obvious. She oftentimes comes across as quiet, shy, and even demure. No one would suspect her until she comes out of her shell and the real nastiness of her perversions are exposed. Undercover, covert hoes are the most dangerous hoes because they are especially good at using deceptive tactics. These hoes have untreated venereal diseases that unsuspecting partners would never guess she would be infected with. They tell their boyfriends that he's their first lover, all the while lying about the fact that they've had 50 others before him. He believes her every word because there is no way this sweet, studious, church going girl, would get down like that.

The daughters' of pastors are probably some of the best examples of undercover hoes. These vixens will be sleeping with all the men in the church. Choir rehearsal is an ideal place to hook-up with an undercover church hoe. Many hoes have a "take it or leave it" attitude when it comes to her treatment of men. In the shadows of the feminist movement and women's rights movements, women are becoming more and more relaxed about their sexual lifestyles and partners. If she gets the urge to do the nasty, she can almost guarantee that some man will be available to satisfy her every need.

Seasoned hoes have no problem treating a man like a used up piece of tissue paper once she's finished with him. The interesting thing about hoes who actually get paid for hoeing is that many people believe that the hoe is one that is at a disadvantage and the one that is being used. In some cases, this is true, but in many cases, the well paid hoe is the one doing the victimizing, swindling thirsty men out of hundreds, even thousands, of dollars at a time. Their rationale in taking these men's money is that if the men are willing to pay them for what most women will do for free, or at least for a cheeseburger, they may as well do it and get paid. Hoes make men's thought processes stop and men who fraternize with hoes aren't good at making decisions. Their whole objective is to indulge in whatever feels good.

Look at Tiger Woods and the types of hoes that were appealing to him. Tiger Woods' had the epitome of what the ideal family and lifestyle is supposed to look like. He had a successful career, wealth, a loving wife, and two small children. He figured out a way to throw it all away over a plethora of hoes that he could not and would not resist. What is it about a hoe that makes a man be willing to lose everything of what should be considered important in his life (family, money, reputation, etc.)? There probably isn't a "good" explanation you can come up with, but it's probably safe to say that booty is a powerful drug.

Hoes just don't have dysfunctional relationships with men. They have some extremely negative relationships with women as well. In many instances, hoes do not get along with other women and they can't stand hoes that are more successful than them. It is utterly ridiculous to imagine being jealous of another female because she is more prolific in degrading herself. Unfortunately, this is the case with a lot of these women. Hoes are jealous of other women that are involved in stable relationships.

Oftentimes, hoes will flirt and sleep with her friend's man just to see if she can break up their relationship. She may not even find her friend's man attractive, she's merely jealous of the fact that her friend is emotionally involved with a man. This emotion is what the hoe lacks in her own life, so her attitude is: if she doesn't have it nobody around me will have it. Lastly, there are segments of the hoe population that actually can't identity or admit that they are hoes yet they will judge and even condemn other women who act just like them. It's fascinating to hear a hoe talk trash about another hoe as though the other hoe's behavior is more deplorable than hers. The men that are involved with these women have either one of two intentions. Men either want a hoe just strictly for his own sexual satisfaction or he desires to make her into a housewife.

The latter scenario is, by far, the more challenging one. Men who attempt to make a hoe into a housewife usually find out the hard way that it is a damn near impossible task. Even if the hoe is on her best behavior for years, all it takes is a stressful or traumatic event in her life to cause her to revert back to her old hoe-like ways.

No matter how hard she tries to adhere to the boundaries of faithfulness and monogamy, in time, most lifelong hoes cannot handle the stress of being with just one man. It takes a certain type of man to deal with the baggage a hoe

brings to a relationship.   Either he will permit her

behavior and allow her to have the freedom to

engage in whatever activities that she wants, or

he will be a hurt and devastated victim and learn

the hard way how difficult it is to make a hoe into

a housewife

Chapter 3

The Classy Bitch

If you want to be around a bitch that is never dull or boring, you may want to hang out with a classy bitch. This bitch is the personification of interesting because every aspect of her life revolves around influence, power, and appearance. Every move that she makes, every step that she takes, is an opportunity that this bitch will take to "pop her collar". The difference between a rich bitch and a classy bitch, is that the classy bitch doesn't necessarily have to have a whole lot of money at her disposal. She can be classy with hundreds of dollars, instead of millions. A classy bitch loves to surround herself with other classy bitches. She will not tolerate spending too much time with unrefined, hood-acting women that act beneath her.

Other people see her as snobbish, conceited, or bourgeoisie. The same is not necessarily true of the men she chooses to hang around. Her man could be an unrefined thug, as long as he's putting her on a pedestal and treating her like a queen. Another important requirement for the man of a classy bitch is that it doesn't matter so much what his personality is like, as long as he can help finance her ability to maintain a lifestyle of influence. Rest assured, a man that deals with a classy bitch will darn near have to marry her in order to get in between her legs. No one night stand shenanigans will work with these classy women. She has standards and men must function within her standards if he wants to be with her.

Classy bitches will do whatever it takes to floss. If that means working 2 jobs to be able to afford living in an affluent part of town, that's the sacrifice she is more than willing to make. If she has to be in a relationship with a man who has a certain level of power and influence in order to have access to these perks, that's not a problem. Women are drawn to men who have power. Take a look at Barack Obama, Bill Clinton, senators, judges, professional athletes, actors, etc. If he is rich and famous, that lifestyle comes with a certain amount of influence. Classy or "wanna-be" classy bitches are drawn to these men like moths to a flame. Her mindset revolves around maintaining a standard.

If she drinks, a classy bitch will not drink cheap stuff. She's not drinking $4 wine; her wine is exclusive and is delivered to her home monthly from her wine club. Everything is the top of the line with her. If's it's not the absolute best, she will pout, make a scene, and demand the best, or she'll just simply do without. Women who have class are usually somewhat educated. They've spent a certain amount of time educating themselves on elegance and grandeur, either through formal education or on topics she's researched on her own. She is well-spoken and knowledgeable in a wide variety of subject matter.

Classy bitches are not ignorant by any means. You can bet, if a classy bitch doesn't know something, she'll make an effort to get information and educate herself on matters that are important to her. She is appearance motivated, meaning there are just some things a classy bitch will be seen in. You could not give a classy bitch a raggedy car to drive even if it was given to her for free. She would rather take a cab to work every day than be seen in a broken down looking vehicle. Her children will not go to public school if the classy bitch can help it. They'll be enrolled in Montessori schools and private schools where they will be able to reflect the same high level of standards that Mommy tries to live by.

All in all, being classy takes a certain amount of discipline and focus. You can't be caught slipping and still expect to remain a classy bitch. If caught slipping, whoever is watching will waste no time talking about how ugly the fall was. To go from classy to hood rat is not a good look. This is why every precaution is made to maintain class status: by any means necessary.

The Self-Righteous Bitch

To others, the self-righteous bitch appears to have it all together. She is moral, spiritual, and all things good. She prides herself on having good conduct and character, and she is typically known among family and friends as a "Miss Goody Two-shoe." To actually believe that a self-righteous bitch is capable of purposeful wrong-doing is an insult to her. Trust and believe, most self-righteous bitches are far from good. She's slightly different from a fake bitch, in that the fake bitch doesn't spend too much time putting other people down while she's living in her fake world.

Self-righteous bitches spend good, quality time castigating other peoples' behavior while she's involved in either the same or very similar behaviors. I've heard these hypocrites talk about how horrible it is and how morally bankrupt a woman has to be to sleep with a married man. She'll then turn around, later in the week, and leave the club early with friends to go hook up for a "quickie" with somebody else's husband! If you call her on it, she'll use some ridiculous excuse to justify her actions, i.e. the married man's wife is dying from cancer and he just needs consolation and a warm breast to lay his head on. She's not only confused about moral issues, self-righteous bitches are spiritual hypocrites too. She goes to church every Sunday, doesn't miss a Bible class, sings on the choir, makes claim to have a close relationship with the Almighty yet; she'll pass by a homeless man, not give him a dime, and surmise that the reason why he is in the shape he is in is because he's lacks a personal relationship with God.

She is good at judging other people's lives and comparing their lives to hers. She is quick to conclude that her life, her actions, her choices, and her decisions have all been the difference between her successes and other peoples' failures. She tends to elevate herself to high heights so that she can degrade others, all in an effort to make herself feel superior. Of all the bitches, she is probably the hardest one to understand because you never can really understand how she justifies how she feels with what she does. Nothing makes sense with this perpetual hypocrite. It's not like she's skillful or even crafty at hiding her less than sanctimoniousness behavior. For these reasons, the self-righteous bitch almost always leaves her family and friends shaking their head in utter disbelief and confusion.

The Smart Bitch

Smart bitches are unique because she's either book smart, street smart, or a little bit of both. The book smart bitch knows something about everything. She's a walking encyclopedia and usually has a few letters behind her name.

Her degrees range from Bachelor to P.H.D., and she is competent within the scope of her study. She's well read and studious and takes educational opportunities very seriously. Even though her relationship with a man is important to her, she is not 100% focused on men. Her attention and energy goes toward building her career and establishing a foundation for a comfortable lifestyle.

Unless you are a bookroom yourself, it's a challenge hanging around this type of bitch. She tends to be extremely analytical and every decision is thoroughly thought out before she decides to execute. Think about how hard it is trying to club hop with an analytical bookworm. Nothing is spontaneous; instead of dancing and heavy hard core drinking, you may be stuck at the bar discussing macroeconomics over a strawberry daiquiri. Intellectually smart bitches are, unsurprisingly, attracted to smart men. If she has her Bachelor's degree, she prefers that her man have one too. Of course, she'll settle for less but not much less. A woman with a Masters' has even higher expectations in her man. A bitch with a P.H.D. is looking for a man with his Doctorate. If he doesn't have one, he'd better be a professional athlete, or he'd better be on television doing something. Otherwise, his chances of being with a highly degreed bitch will be slim.

Not all smarts have anything to do with books. Hanging with a street smart sidekick can sometimes mean the difference between life and death. Having fun and going out can sometimes be harmful to your health and knowing what clubs to go to at a certain times of day or night will help keep you out of all sorts of compromising situations. Knowing who to socialize with and being aware of verbal and nonverbal dangers are what separates street smart bitches from all others. Her instincts are keen and she's good at reading other peoples' verbal and nonverbal cues.

A street smart bitch can help get you out of sticky life situations .Her tendency toward thuggish ways is sexy to a lot of men. Some men love the fact that their woman will, if she had to, go toe to toe in an instant with any adversary she may cross paths with. In all honesty, it's hard to find anyone better than a woman who has both book and street smarts. This combination forms the foundation of one

powerful mate. If you can find her, consider

yourself lucky because you've found yourself a

gem. A woman who has both is a diamond in the

ruff in the truest sense.

Chapter 4

The Dumb Bitch

If you want to have a life filled with headaches and frustration, hang around one of these bitches. If you look up the word "dumb', Webster defines it as, 'lacking the human power of speech". There are a few other definitions but none pertain to the meaning referred to in this book. A dumb bitch lacks most, if not all, of the qualities that smart bitches possess. There aren't too many people that will get you killed like hanging around a dumb bitch will. She's the type that insist on taking the bus and train to the raunchiest nightspot in town. Once there, she'll order 10 shots of Patron over the course of 2-3 hours. As the night goes on and she gets more and more inebriated, she begins to get

boisterous and rowdy with all the women in the

club, and even some of the men. All that

mischief-making doesn't stop her from picking up

one of the men, taking him in the alley, and

having unprotected sex with him. Before you

realize she's even gone, she's stumbling back

into the club and announces that, after all that,

she's ready to go home. As you're leaving, the

bartender informs the dumb bitch that her card

has been declined and that he needs another

method of payment for those 10 shots of tequila.

As her companion, you reach into your pocket

and settle the tab so that you can be free to

leave. Low and behold, it's 4 a.m. and no buses

are running to get back to the train to go home.

So you and the dumb bitch have to walk the

streets of this treacherous neighborhood all alone to make the last train. Luckily, you had enough sense to carry cash so now you're on the train listening to her apologize for costing you an extra 100 bucks and an entire night of aggravation. The moral of the story is: never hang out with dumb bitches.

There are a few instances where dumb bitches actually are pretty knowledgeable people. How can that be? Everyone knows at least one woman who has her master's degree, or P.H.D., but who has a boyfriend that sits at her home all day playing video games. Not only does she permit him to play video games, she actually really loves him for reasons that, even she, can't coherently explain. She loves this man's dirty underwear. This dumb bitch has a successful career, owns her own home, drives a beautiful car, and has great credit. She could have any of a number of men, but for some unexplained reason, she chooses to take care of a free-loading, lazy bum. In her mind, she knows she can do better, but her ever-growing low self-esteem keeps her putting up with his madness.

For his part, men like this know full well what kind of woman he has, and he knows just what to do (and what not to do) to keep her. He'll succumb to a little cooking and cleaning but going out and getting a job is definitely not an option. He's fully aware of her dumb bitch tendencies, and he relies on the fact that he's smart enough to get as much as he can, for as long as he can. His justification being: if I don't use her, somebody else will.

The Gold Digger Bitch

It doesn't matter where you live in the world, on whatever continent, no matter her color or creed, everyone knows someone who is a gold-digging bitch. The name speaks for itself. This bitch loves anything associated with money. She'll sleep with any man, or any woman, as long as she can get her paws on their pocketbooks. She devises the best tailor made plans geared toward the man that she intends to dig. She shows her victims' pocketbook no mercy and she will stop at nothing to get what she wants. What does the gold digging bitch want? She wants money and access to anything that has monetary value. What makes a gold-digger different than a rich bitch is that a gold-digger is on the constant lookout for more riches. She gets her riches from outside sources, not from her own earnings, and that's the point. Gold diggers do not desire to work for their money in order to maintain their lifestyles. They insist on someone else providing for them. That is their full time job. They could very well have another job, but gold-digging is at the top of their "to-do list".

Gold diggers are not always obvious and easily detectable. I know a woman in her 40's who owns a successful insurance company, has her own home, and she lives a relatively comfortable lifestyle. She is, however, a gold-digging machine. This bitch ONLY dates men who are, without exception, 70 years old and over. She's attractive, is educated, and only has one child (who's in college, by the way). She could have her choice of man, but she does not want a man, she's after the money. Any 70 year old man will not do.

This 70 year man has a fantastic pension, gets social security, and works a part time job at Home Depot. Together, this old man brings in over $15,000 a month. You're probably asking yourself why a man who generates $15,000 a month works a part time job. The answer is: to pay for his gold-digging bitch! Remember, he has two households to maintain, his household and her household. There is little doubt that this feeble man is not aware that he's being played. The fact is: he does not care that he's being taken advantage of. The mere fact that a young, beautiful, intelligent, sweet-smelling woman is paying good attention to him is enough for him.

Gold-digging bitches seek a variety of money welding men. She prefers athletes. Professional athletes are money dripping, ego thirsty maniacs and are usually ripe for the taking. All she has to do is look relatively presentable, treat him like an oil king, and be able to sodomize him to the best of her ability. These three assets are a requirement for these bitches to successfully gold-dig these men. Once a gold-digger snarls her victim, he has a decision to make. Marrying a gold digging bitch can prove to be a devastating life decision. Her desires for wealth and prosperity are especially dangerous for particularly old husbands of gold-digging bitches.

Unless she's a compassionate digger or if she actually does have feeling for the old man, he should watch her closely.   As soon as they return from their Vegas nuptials, his clock starts ticking. Old men who are either wealthy with assets, or who have large life insurance policies, are prime targets for these women. Diggers that prey on these men know that all they have to do is blow their old geezerr a few kisses and rub on his penis every now and then. In their minds, that is enough and should secure their inheritance. Sure it's selfish and cruel- hearted, but it works and that is all that matters to these gold digging bitches.

The Mean Bitch

A woman is usually a mean bitch on a regular basis, or she's an intermittent mean bitch. There are women in the world who walk around angry and mean, not just sometimes, but damn near all the time. They exude unhappiness and discontent with their own lives and unto the lives of everyone around them. Everything a mean bitch says, does, and even thinks, is negative. Mean bitches use foul language all the time and their vocabulary is usually very limited. Even in casual conversation, it's hard to leave a conversation with her feeling positive. She will bring the spirit down of everyone around her so mean bitches either tend to have very few friends, or the friends she does have, are mean bitches themselves.

There are some who would argue that every woman on the planet could, at one time or another, be classified as a mean bitch. This is true, as we all have our moments, but what separates mean bitches from every other kind of bitch is their ability to turn on their meanness when it is totally unnecessary. For instance, I was a waitress at a popular seafood restaurant some years ago. I waited on a young woman and her husband who, at first, were great guests. The husband ordered a soup as an appetizer and both of them ordered entrees. For some reason, I forgot to bring out the husband's soup. As I was delivering their main dishes, the wife turns to me and says, "Is this your day job?" Confused by her question, I naively answered, "Yes." She then proceeds to remind me that I had forgotten her husband's soup and how unforgiveable that was. She starts ranting and raving about how horrible I was and that I had ruined their whole dining experience. At this point, I start profusely apologizing because the last thing I wanted to do was make their experience a bad one and mess up my chances of earning an even worse tip.

She quieted down and everything else went smoothly. They finished their meal and asked for their check. I dropped their check off at the table, again apologizing for my mistake, and even offering to bring them a complimentary soup to take home. The husband pays the check and leaves me a $15 cash tip; I saw it on the table as I processed his credit card.   They leave the restaurant and I return back to the table to retrieve the tip. Here's where the second part of the mean bitch moment occurred. As I approach the table, I look and instead of the $15, I see a penny and a note that read, "Next time, don't forget my husband's soup!" Who else would do something like that but an ultra bitch! I shook my head, regained my composure, and finished the rest of my shift believing that she would eventually pay for her treatment of me. Sometimes it's easy to spot a mean bitch from a mile away. Some of them have a certain look to them that cannot be mistaken. They love to roll their eyes, turn up their lips, and they're especially effective at looking older than their actual age. Meanness has a way of aging a person; they do not realize that just a tiny morsel of niceness can go a long, long way.

Chapter 5

The Ghetto-Fabulous Bitch

Although the word "ghetto"' is frequently used to describe a slum or a poor, crime-ridden neighborhood, "ghetto" is also used to describe the mindset of a people. When someone calls a person "ghetto", they are trying to convey the idea that the person they are referring to acts like a product of their low class and violent environments. A ghetto bitch or hood-rat, is violent, inarticulate, low-class, and low maintenance. Very few ghetto bitches admit to being one. Ghetto bitches do not even realize how ghetto that they are and deny their ghetto fabulous tendencies.

However, if you were to ask anyone who spends any amount of time with her, they would emphatically include her without hesitation. Why? Because ghetto bitches can't hide their attitudes and emotions very easily. If she gets upset or angry, a ghetto bitch has very little discipline to be able to keep her emotions under control. If she's pissed, everyone will know it and she will not care about how she is perceived by other people. She is a master at using foul language in public, and she prefers that as many people as possible are in earshot of her profanity. Ghetto bitches stand out like sore thumbs. They drive cheap, souped-up cars with rims, and you can usually hear them coming from a mile away from all the loud music.

Men who love hood-rats are a unique breed themselves. They are thrill-seeking weaklings who like the adventure that spending time with a ghetto bitch provides for them. Every day is unusual, bold, and even risky because her behavior is often unpredictable. For ghetto bitches, her look is always "extra". She can't just wear braids. Her braids have to have the extra strand of color added to them, i.e. green, fuchsia, blue, or purple. She believes her look is uniquely original but she does not realize that it's uniquely "ghetto". Of course, when she's called on her distasteful look, she'll accuse you of being a hater in a heartbeat.

The Gossiping Bitch

This bitch is a big mouth who cannot hold water. If you ever want your business kept under wraps, you may want to steer clear from this type of bitch. She has an almost uncontrollable urge to tell everybody's business to any and everybody she comes into contact with. Nobody is safe from her nosiness and her big mouth. If she has information that is supposed to be kept a secret, she'll take great pride in disclosing the secret and she'll even believe that she's doing the world a favor in doing so.

Gossiping bitches can be found in almost any arena. They are prevalent in the workplace, at church, in school, and pretty much anywhere where people are allowed to gather and speak.

For this reason, it is hard to get away from women with diarrhea of the mouth, but there are ways to handle the ones that you may come in contact with. One of the most effective ways of handling a gossiping bitch is to simply walk away from her. The moment she starts running her mouth, take off on her. Don't let her finish her sentence and don't give her the attention she seeks. Before she knows it, she'll be left standing there talking to herself and wondering why she's been left alone to do so.   These women seek attention and power so they act like human newspapers, spreading both good and slanderous information. You'll rarely see or hear a gossiping bitch talk about her own personal or private affairs. If she does talk about her own life, rest assured, it is in the most glowing terms.

Gossiper's favorite topics are about who so-in-so is sleeping with and what all the juicy details she was able to find out about it. She loves to be the first to spread the news about other people's misfortune; from foreclosures to pregnancy news, this bitch has the scoop and is eager to tell whoever will listen all about it.

The Manipulative Bitch

This is the bitch that people all over the world need to be on the lookout for. She is cunning, shrewd, and calculating. Her goal is to change the perception or behavior of others through underhanded, deceptive, or even abusive methods. She can easily be mistaken for a mean bitch, however, there are a few differences. The mean bitch is usually more one dimensional in her outward expression of discontent. The manipulative bitch uses more complex tactics to achieve her desired goals.

Master manipulating bitches will generally take the time to scope out the characteristics and vulnerabilities of their victim. Once they identify where their victim is vulnerable, they pounce on them like a wild cat. Most of their prey are either naïve or emotionally dependent people. Their naïve victims find it too hard to accept the idea that some people are cunning, devious and ruthless or they are "in denial" that he or she is even being victimized. Manipulative women seek out emotionally dependent victims because they have a submissive or dependent personality. The more emotionally dependent the victim is, the more vulnerable he or she is to being exploited and manipulated. What do manipulative bitches want? Their desires may vary, but they almost always have a need to advance their own purposes and personal gain and will do so at virtually any cost to others.

They have a strong desire to attain feelings of superiority in their relationships and they like to be the one in control. Her man is, for the most part, unsuspecting and unaware of her antics. I've seen a female family member use her body and her temper to manipulate her man out of all sorts of favors. If she wants a new stove, she'll prepare home cooked meals every day for weeks, then she'll, all of a sudden, claim the stove is broken. Once she gets the new stove, she'll whine about how she doesn't want to overuse it and insist that he take her out to dinner every night. She not only gets to decorate her kitchen with the newest model stove, she also gets to not use it and eat out every night, which was her intention all along. The clear intentions of these skillful dupers is never revealed until it's too late which means that over a lifetime, these manipulators are sure to have multiple victims left in their past.

Chapter 6

The Steal Your Man Bitch

Every effort this bitch puts forth is focused on possessing who and what belongs to someone else. It doesn't matter if a genuine interest in the man is there or not, as long as he belongs to someone else, she is interested. For obvious reasons, the steal your man bitch is definitely into married men. She adores married men and has a sexual attraction to them that even she cannot explain. She's especially drawn to married men who wear their wedding rings and who talk about their wives in glowing terms. These men are a challenge to her and she will use every tool in her arsenal to snarl that man.

If she works with him, she'll dress provocatively and take great care in making sure that her appearance is her focal point. She'll wear dresses that subtly reveal her cleavage, skirts or pants that show off her curvy hips and butt, and 4" heels that show off her pedicured toes. Every opportunity she gets, she's always in her married co-worker's face asking him stupid questions about something or another. She makes sure to stand unnecessarily close to him to insure he gets a whiff of her perfume, or she'll make certain that he can smell the scented aroma of her hair. The steal your man bitch is very calculating when it comes to single men who have a girlfriend too. She will go after him in much the same way as the married man. She is not interested in single men who aren't in relationships because these men present no challenge for her. She wants the man who is in love with someone else. He presents the challenge because if she can get him to sleep with her and even leave his wife or girlfriend, only then can her ego be nourished and fed.

Chances are, the steal your man bitch doesn't even want to be in a relationship with the man, all she wants is the challenge of taking somebody else's man away from their perceived stable relationship. Most of these women have no respect for themselves and have issues with both women and men. They are filled with jealousy and envy toward their women peers, and they have deep seated hatred for men. They view men as pawns in their game of love chess.

Married men are despicable to her and she puts forth every effort available to her to destroy him once she cuffs him. She's the type that, after she sleeps with a married man, will call his wife and inform her of all the gory details of her rendezvous with her husband. There have been times where the steal your man bitch has been known to fall in love with the man that she has successfully stolen. The man that was a super challenge and difficult to lure away from his girl, or the one that she had to pull out all the stops to seduce are the types of men that the SYM bitch would fall head over heels for. You can compare her to a fisherman out on the lake who catches a fish, if it were an easy catch, he'll throw it back in the water. If he had to wait all day to catch it, he'll keep it to enjoy later. So is, the mindset of the steal your man bitch.

The Trifling Bitch

I am almost certain that everybody has come across this type of bitch at least one time or another. By definition, trifling means "frivolous or lacking significance". However, for the sake of how it is most widely defined in slang terms, it means to be lazy, shiftless, and filthy. Growing up, most females have heard their mothers' warm them against turning into one of these types of bitches. This is the type of bitch nobody wants to be. But no matter how hard a woman tries not to be trifling, there are some who will fall through the trifling cracks. In your teens, your mother may accuse you of trifling behavior for doing things like not flushing the toilet after using it or not picking up dirty underwear off of the floor after showering. These are minor infractions. As she gets older, trifling bitches are guilty of far more disgusting offenses. Most people know of at least one member of their family or friend that has made her evolution into this category of bitches.

Although it's easy to recognize a trifling bitch on sight, her identity is usually solidified when you take one look at her children and/or the inside of her home. Let's examine the condition of the children first. A trifling bitch's children are generally in bad shape. She does very little to care for them and it is apparent in their appearance. On any given day, she'll send her children to school with their hair not cleaned or combed, their clothes not clean or pressed, and they will be without food or anything to sustain them throughout the day. Some may mistake being trifling with being poor. There are some extenuating factors that contribute to both, but they are not the same. I've seen poor women who can't afford new clothes for their children, yet their children still are clean and well maintained. What makes a mother especially trifling is when her children are filthy and neglected, but she is the epitome of glamorous.

Unfortunately, there are too many bitches that fit this description running around our planet and not enough people calling them out on this behavior. Another dead giveaway of a trifling bitch can sometimes be revealed when you step one foot in her home. One of the last things you want to do is eat a meal in a trifling bitch's home. Her home is as filthy as she is. She cares very little about cleanliness and her lack of self-pride shows in the upkeep of her home. The most thing about a trifling woman is her ability to snag a man. Albeit, he is probably just as trifling as she is, the fact that she can still find a man willing to deal with her is truly unbelievable. I have seen men have sex with, date, and even marry these women as if it is acceptable to be involved with filth. On the positive note, trifling behavior can be corrected with a slight shift in attitude and the use of soap, some bleach, and some water.

The Jealous Bitch

Most people struggle with this particular character flaw at one time or another in their lives. Jealousy and envy are normal feelings that will creep into the heart of even the most well-meaning individual. The key to combating these emotions is to fight against them when they occur. Fighting back is something the consistently jealous bitch has trouble doing. It's understandable to be jealous of a person that has something or someone that you would love to have. The struggle comes when that jealousy turns to evil thoughts about the other person. When jealous bitches begin to plan and plot against the people they are jealous of, that is where the line is drawn.

Why is it hard for jealous bitches to want for other people what they desire for themselves? Little do they realize that once she let's go of feelings of insecurity, fear, and anxiety, those feeling will flee from her and open her up to her own blessings in life. This is a hard concept for jealous hearted people to understand. They would rather drink the "hatorade" and plot against the success of other individuals. Jealousy can occur in just about every aspect of human life. Fat bitches are jealous of skinny bitches. Poor bitches are jealous of rich bitches. Single bitches are jealous of married bitches. The lists can go on and on for an eternity which is why it all doesn't make any sense. When women realize that all attributes can either be characterized as "good" or "bad", it becomes much easier to just accept, love, and if all else fails, just be yourself.

The Lazy Bitch

Looking back, the lazy bitch can easily be included in any one of the other types of bitches. A tiny aspect of laziness can be found in every other type. So what makes a lazy bitch exclusively stand out in this particular category? The answer is simple: a lazy bitch has no drive, no ambition, no motivation, and she downright refuses to do anything to improve any aspect of her life. Lazy bitches make life miserable for everyone around them. Just ask anyone that works with a lazy bitch. She can come to work, punch in the clock, and literally sit at her desk all day doing one of three things. She's either eating all day, gossiping on the telephone, or taking cat naps when nobody is looking. This woman is totally unapologetic about the fact that she may be causing other people at work more stress and strain. Her co-workers have to make up for the work that she refuses to do.

The irony is that most lazy bitches seek jobs that they know they can get away with this type of behavior. They choose jobs that allow them the opportunity to remain inconspicuous, i.e. government positions, security positions, clerical work, etc. Many lazy bitches don't even have jobs. They may give a number of different excuses as to why they're not employed but never will they admit the obvious reason. By definition, lazy means to be disinclined to do work or to exert energy. Hence, there are possibly millions of women all over the world right now that do not have jobs, not because they're unqualified and not because of lack of available jobs. These bitches don't have jobs because they are slothful and lazy. Their biggest obstacle in life is their lack of self-motivation. They're also idle-minded in many other areas of their life. For instance, because she will refuse to exercise, a lazy bitch is usually overweight. She will make no effort to even prepare and cook her own food. Everything she eats is either take-out food or it's warmed up in a microwave. Her home is not well kept because cleaning is just not a daily regimen that lazy bitches take seriously.

Many lazy bitches oftentimes wonder why they can't keep a man. She does not realize that one of the worse places to act lazy is in the bedroom. No real man wants a woman that lays flat on her back and won't move a muscle during sex. Unfortunately, lazy bitches do just that, all the while complaining about being tired and sleepy. After 1 or 2 episodes of boring sex, the man is fed up and ends the relationship. The irony is that lazy bitches like to complain about how there aren't any good man in the world. The solution lies within her; all she has to do is quit being so lazy and just move something!

Bitches with Problems

The rapper Jay-Z said it best in a rap song entitled, "99 Problems". Bitches with problems are a common occurrence in today's society. With so many things happening in the world, it's not unlikely to have problems on top of problems. To have the mental strength to handle so many life issues is remarkable. Bitches can sometimes cause a lot of their own misfortunes but, for the most part, things can just happen beyond the scope of your control. I know bitches who have financial problems, man problems, children problems, and health problems. The sad part is, they are not dealing with these problems separately. Many of them are battling all of these issues all at the same time! To complicate and make matters worse, bitches with problems have a hard time finding friends to help them cope with life. To be an effective friend, you would literally have to listen to and provide counseling to your problem-ridden girlfriend. That requires a huge amount of love and patience which are two attributes most people just don't have.   Bitches with problems are usually left on their own to solve and work through them. Because friends are hard to come by, bitches with problems are usually very religious people. They live in church, are always praying, and they love quoting scriptures at any random moment. Some may characterize her actions as "crazy acting", but if you think about it, a bitch with a ton of problems is in pain and is suffering. Prolonged suffering has a way of making any mortal a lunatic. The bitch with problems needs to take whatever steps necessary to alleviate her problems. If she has 10 problems, she should start with one and knock them out one at a time. Some may be harder to get rid of than others, but if she devises a plan to attack them one by one, she may eventually be able to rid herself of them altogether. She can lose the title of "The Bitch with Problems", and can now be known as, "The Bitch with Solutions".

The plight of women all over the world is intriguing and unique. No other species on the planet is fashioned quite like the female. To identify 20 types of bitches in the world barely scratches the surface to the infinite amount of bitches that actually exist in the world. She possesses so many characteristics that it would be near impossible to encapsulate all of them in one book. The interesting part about exploring these 20 types of bitches is that the more bitches you explore, the more types of bitches become unveiled. With the unveiling of the "new" bitches, I am reminded that within every bitch, therein lies her opposite expression. This expression is the hope and desire of the whole of mankind. Later bitches!

Other Books Available By Author On Kindle, Audio and Paperback

The Mind Games Women Play On Men